Kibbe

For Becky,
Warmest Regards

For my sisters and Betty Jo

Kibbe

Poems by
Suzan Azar Porterfield

Mayapple Press 2012

Published by   MAYAPPLE PRESS
                 362 Chestnut Hill Rd.
                 Woodstock, NY 12498
                 www.mayapplepress.com

ISBN 978-1-936419-08-1

ACKNOWLEDGMENTS

Beirut Redux, Between Two Worlds, *Le Journal des Poetes* (2009), Christine Pagnoulle, trans.; Connecticut Girl in Love, Recognizing the Olive, *Flyway* (2008); Sometimes the Dead Choose to Reappear, *Caesura* (spring 2008); The House in Kousba, Inshalla, Ahmed and Me, *theKerf* (2008); The Mountains of Lebanon, The Last Azars in Kousba, Eid al-Fatir, Phoenician Alphabet, *Nimrod* (spring/summer 2007); Lebanon, *Crab Orchard Review* 9.2 (Summer/Fall 2004); Kibbe, *North American Review* (March-April 2003); Beach Road to Miramar Resort, anthologized in *Imagine Peace* (Bottom Dog Press 2009); Terrorist, Beirut, anthologized in *Poetry on the Lake* (Wyvern Works Press 2008, England); *Beirut Redux* (FinishingLine Press 2008); Arabic Lesson, *In the Garden of Our Spines* (Mayapple Press 2004).

Thanks to John Bradley, Joe Gastiger, Ric Amesquita, Becky Parfitt. And, as always, to Christopher.

Cover photo by Amal Haig. Cover designed by Judith Kerman. Book designed and typeset by Amee Schmidt with cover titles in Gaze, poem titles in High Tower Text, and text in Adobe Garamond Pro. Author photo courtesy of Christopher Porterfield.

Contents

/

/

/

"Don't write history as poetry"

—Mahmoud Darwish

Kibbe

Today in the land of new-world corn,
heart of the Midwest, I'm making kibbe.

I'll need pine nuts and minced lamb,
cinnamon bark from an East India tree,

and bulghur, which my father called,
as I do, by its Arabic name.

The sound slips from my tongue,
and already onion and pignolias,

allspice, butter-browned, scent the house.
Already I'm wrapped in the alleys

of Beirut where murmurs drift from kitchens
of women who look like me.

Our genius is in the dish,
and in the dish made word.

Years ago, oil and figs, papyrus
and purple dye sailed from Byblos

to Athens to Rome. Now *olive,*
bread, wine can send us reeling.

Someone is always making kibbe.
Tomorrow a daughter in Damascus

will make it. The day after,
a mother in Jenin.

Between Two Worlds

(for Alfred George Azar)

Asleep,
I glimpse the face
of your hand,
trail a trace
of your back
along a darkened hall,
but you spill
into shade.

If you
will come again,
I promise
to keep up.
You must be wanting
to lead me home.

Lebanon

The land of the father is remembered
by the child, fruited in flesh and eye,

sweetmeat of fig, oil of almond
pressed from skins to her tongue,

blessing her back to a path lined
with almond, fig, to a limestone house

she's not seen and knows as she knows
the mountains at dawn, how they lift

to shadow the ocean, or the breath
of the Bekka Valley, asleep. That

is a country of myth. The young die
in each other's arms and somewhere,

a relic shoe or cane amidst ash.
That is a country called old by the father

of she who longs to sail for its shores,
cast nets like searchlights on water,

this daughter of sesame and rose,
of the cedar axed to the root.

Sometimes the Dead Choose to Reappear

It either is or is not you
as the plane lowers into Beirut.

Either I am or am not alone.
Only you would know.

At Heathrow by the Limbo gate,
everyone's speaking Arabic

except me, who may or
may not be going home.

In Chicago, remember, at the A&P
to tease us, your girls,

you'd fish a pickle from a jar,
then replace it on the shelf?

You were our dad, but
we'd pretend you weren't.

Now, here, as the plane regains earth,
and no one remains seated,

ignoring the attendant's plea,
it's either you I hear laughing,

or it's me.

Beirut Redux

Let her be courtesan, scholar, or saint . . .
—Nadia Tuéni

Some verandas, like strings of pearls,
still drape the chests of gray, shell-pocked homes.

At dusk, blinded windows front the dark strolling up
like a lover you tried to forget.

Beirut burns to bury her past, to arise
a *once-there-was* virgin lass,

waist airy as grass and whole
as the schoolgirls in jeans or hijabs

who lean at the university's gate.
Meanwhile, in fitful streets,

above nightclubs, above rival taxi horns,
the muezzin's *Allahu akhbar* hums,

and Starbucks opens careful doors . . .

Turn a bright corner—

diamonds spotless in new storefront glass,
and there's another of those old whores,

its bombed-out doorway a musky hole,
whispering a come-on in the ear.

We in the Middle

(from this side one wave rolls in,
from that side another, and we in the middle . . .)
　　　　—Alcaeus

Beyond that heart of Lebanon's shore,
Syria's there. Sometimes, at night,
over arak and mountain, narcotic air,
we rouse ourselves. We call out,

"Syria again," "Syria tonight" and sail on.
Cousins and friends warn of drifting too far south,
past Sidon, close by the border where Israel,
uncharted isle, spins Cyclops jets

across our bow. *I cannot tell where the wind lies.*
Hurry, we must strengthen the ship's sides
against the coming storm.
I've seen winter swells smash over walls,

eyeballs white as foam, branching legs and arms
snapped on a fragile land. Like pebbles, like leaves,
like children washed from their mother's arms,
we are dragged back and back and down.

Greenline

*. . . as if the heat of the sun had boiled and fried all the glories of
the earth into a single mess.*
—*Forster,* Passage to India

In summery blaze, landscape weeps
like a cracked egg, pomegranates

glaze into candy, casinos and cafés burn.
Noontimes on the veranda,

clinking icy gin, I overlook the sea
luminous as a lapis lazuli sky

and expect, as if a dream,
the horizon's ridge. Now I see,

it's mist and chill reveals it,
that greenline trace, the edge.

"Remember—the noise of moonlight"

—"In the Lebanese Mountains," Nadia Tuéni

Scorpion

Seahorse, I thought
though straight off that seemed wrong.
Its back end curled strangely,
and the kitchen drawer we both
had at that moment claimed
was far from shore.

Maybe it's dead.
The notion cheered me
as I skimmed a breath across its length,
hoping I'd found a corpse.
It scratched edgeways a bit
like a sleep-stubborn, teenage boy,
and I thought how I wished
it'd been a seahorse after all, those toys—
like dollhouse toasters and phones—
ponies you could ride
almost, grabbing hold, flying off
in a kingdom beneath the waves.

      I remembered hearing
about an explorer who wouldn't go on.
Tent-bound, he waited at the snowy base camp
for his comrades' return, and snug in his bag,
slept all day or read an adventure tale
about a journey to the very place he was.

Two days after I'd trapped my beast
and sent it packing,
padding barefoot about my darkened flat,
I hitch-stepped over another not-a-seahorse guest
and was witness to its whirligigged tail.

Parable of Driving in Lebanon

Wife run off, the baby too,
he no longer does the dishes or shaves.
Not for weeks.

In whatever niche will fit,
he drops his body down to sleep—
a chair, a bathroom floor.

After all, what law says *Bed?*
Bed, he sees, is up to him alone.
So is *Dinner, Clean Socks,*

Too Fast, One-Way Street and *Yield.*
        Who knew?
Who knew the love he'd die for,

mist and a flash of glass?
Late for work, he backs his car against
the traffic's flow, flips it

into gear, and won't be stopping
for any damn sign.

Beach Road to Miramar Resort

My driver may have been Hezbollah—
       hard to say,
a young man, serious in that way
some young men here are.

They walk without unraveling,
keeping their eyes below ground. They wait.
For work, for women.
They wait and flare and are not light.

Even his smile, when it came,
tied in as an alien ship.
He understood the way to survive
meant more of my kind

arriving every day.
It's possible he was Hezbollah.
In how he talked—justice, Iraq,
the ones who sacrifice blood.

Why, he asked, did America,
rigid spine of human rights,
shrug at Palestinian pain? *You must not
drink the water,* he advised and stopped

so I could buy three liters-full.
You will need food.
And he stopped again, then unasked,
hauled my suitcases, the burden

of my being, water and groceries
upstairs. He placed them just inside
the door. *You will like it here.*
Open the curtains, he said.

The dark room exploded
in sea-light and a cooling breeze, and yes,
I think, perhaps, he was Hezbollah.

The Mountains of Lebanon

The Tennessee hills are as green with pine and cleave to sky
like these, wedged with towns in slabs amid the slant
of olive groves, grape, and clementine.

I believe my father is in Tennessee,
layered beneath a marble block,
striations of wedged bone, stone, ash.

I believe he's here
in the Kadisha Valley, spirited lightly away,
uprooted as before.

With the Mediterranean on my left, I drive out of Beirut
where I can breathe in
the quilted silence laid down upon these hills,
the ghost-light arising, hearth by hearth, at dusk.

Feeding the Children

(During the Civil War, Lebanon lost almost all of its wildlife.)

I've seen birds fall from trees
behind my flat as the chop
of a gun claps my ear
and later went to look,
expecting almost nothing left.
The birds here are so slight, so few.
Such a pop must surely burst
the delicate breast,
quickening on a limb,
too small even to feed
a child born after war.

Fox

There outside my door, the filigreed print
of the fox driven by the night's storm.
Did she knock?

I would've let her in, we two
curled in hiding from the rabid wind's
hounding down the mountain, its huffing

snout shoved into the cracks of my flat.
Throughout the blast, by candlelight
I crouched alone.

I didn't know she'd tamed herself
to snug against my stoop, which took guts
and cunning, as we've heard.

Doing what it takes to hang on
gets you called sly, I guess,
as if somewhere in the mash

of chance or fate or luck
signs are who they are
only when we open up.

Connecticut Girl in Love

Her burqa hides an ochre rose,
mouth and tongue, blood and skin
coupled upon her neck.

Glad I've come, she unveils
her Mr. Coffee, her Starbuck's stash,
and I see she's forgotten

the bruising hothouse bloom.
In sweat pants, a *Go Patriots* tee
her body tumbles soft and loose

and betrays her husband's joy
at the hush-hush flesh,
the peacock tattoo he's wooed

up from a mother vein,
his need to make visible the seed,
to be rooted, to grip and suck.

Coyotes at Balamand

At dusk in the hills it begins
                    one voice
                              hungry, unworded, and soon
        other yowls choir down
                    from towns sharing bread
                              sharing wine, and soon again
and then
    a howling lifts
                    from an iftaring village, sound summoning
            sound
                    and there's ravenous ringing above
                              and below, and the mountain
turning, is flashing out their crying
                    their calling every night each to each—

            we are here
                              we are here and starved

        oh family

Seashells on Mt. Lebanon

Sometimes you'll find one.
It can see from here its dreamed-of world,
the sea that left it on a swag of sandy floor.

Nothing about an empty shell yearns,
not residue of the living soul
that must have leaned
toward the abandoning blue,
heartbroken to be left all alone—

                I could believe
what it was meant to do
the shell has done,

wait for me
to read myself into its tale.

I take it home and put it on a shelf,
a sign of the hand of a god
who placed it once, just so.

Seeing Saddam's Farmhouse Lair on Satellite T.V. or Even Hitler Loved Dogs

It wasn't so much the curl of her Kurdish arm
around the baby's head,
mother and child succumbing as one,
or the splash of gunshot beyond Council doors.
It wasn't the *you're forgiven, come home*
that doomed the grooms of his girls,
nor even his little fêtes of torture and rape.

It was his Mars Bars made in France
(like the one I was just then munching),
the wrappers friendly, brown and red,
littering the farmhouse floor amid his flip-flops
and new skivvies, two to a pack.

Street Kids

You cannot do in Sydney, Philly,
or Kent what's done here.

Down narrow streets, collectors skim,
bags in hand, fondling the choicest bits

to carry home, sometimes to throw back after.
The luckiest get fed, taught to cook

or speak an English phrase.
These small pearls tossed up,

nacreous stuff, snips of broken shell.
We've read our Nabokov and Mann—

Bellinis on the balcony, Darling,
bijoux in the boudoir.

Phoenician Alphabet

The letter *A* is the (o)mega,
S's (e)vade, the *X* tries not to (of)fend.

Each letter is the gist, offers inside
its Gnostic god alive.

We choose the word for beauty's sake,
one carved mark insisting the next,

consonant, vowel and vowel all
in rapturous sound circling round to beginnings,

as autumn precedes winter or *A* is to *B*,
because for all you know,

I might be dead and on the make,
circumventing time and space. Oh yes,

it's always a surprise.
One day you're reading some silly book,

and a word starts to shake,
and you fall into a faint and speak in tongues

or chant, *Oh God, Oh God, Oh God.*
       Aleph, Alpha, Allah.

Inshaalla

From a perception of only 3 senses . . .
none could deduce a fourth or fifth.
—Blake

From a byte of light in the brain
none could deduce a door.

From a door ajar to the wild
none could deduce a poem.

The shade of the crane, like a poem,
startles the passing fish.

The passing of a fish or its birth
comforts the universal eye.

Before I could read,
letters fell like leaves.

After leaving the open book,
I walked in the world of men.

From the wickedness of men,
no one could deduce a God.

English Flier for "Back to Nature"
Perfumed Soaps, Khan Al Saboun Souk

The soaps are round as ben wa balls,
    softly-colored,
        cuddled each in its paper wrap.
Bins of jasmine blossom, lavender, lily, mint.

      When we use the soap, we must cover the body
      completely with soap and water, then we mix them
      over our body as we make a message there.

There's a message in *message* hard to read:
    we have received? we are part of?
                no lonely men here?
If "letter" or "missive" instead, we'd have read
    "use this soap to make a letter on the body,"
             and it's *lingua*

    that old seducer once again,
though I'd like "showing one's colors" or
             "hail and speak,"
    two bodies (soaped up) like two ships passing,
      you show me your flag, I'll show you mine . . .

      . . . the wisemen assume that the smell is attached
      to the deep breath accompanied with the sexual relation
      the heart beats and harmony.

The word *harmony* here could never mean
    "teamwork"
      or "good vibes," I think, though
"esprit de corps"
somehow inspires—
    but *sexual relation, heart beats,* and "teamwork"?
             No.

Better would be "sweetness,"
      "quiet"
      "peace, "

leading, it might seem, to a corner chair and book
    but goes further, deeper in
        through "symmetry" and "balance" deeper and deeper
            rocking through the body to limb-loosening
"bliss."
                Meaning has its Tantric poses,
    slips in-between, slides underneath,
        likes it rough and edgy,
           would rather be bed
than wed.

Kahil Gibran Museum, Becharré

He too was a little mad,
his wordgroves tended,
like the few cedar trees still tall,
lest all be lost. It's true. Prophet-talk—

it just kills us now.
Though if, like him, I'd had these hills,
perhaps I too could speak from height,
climb more than clutch.

He might've been Blake,
he might've been Barnum, but from him I take this cue:
If in the twilight, *if in the twilight of memory,*
I see a picture in a book of a deeply-lidded eye,

studding the palm of an open, upraised hand,
then something remains. In a childish scrawl,
in the blanks of that, my father's book,
I scribbled prophecies before I could write.

Arabic Lesson

Within the body of this tongue
I believe I lurk, a germ in the blood,
an immigrant gene. Matrix of sound
and script, are you mother
to my bitter laugh and brittle skin?
You're alien, I know, but honey and roses
issue from my mouth even at noon.
I'm the most surprised.

And yet I say:
This. That. The fact is.

And yet I dream,
wandering ships on bluest seas.

"A real country, not a metaphor . . ."

—"We Walk on the Bridge," Mahmoud Darwish

Why We Travel

I am not here in Kousba;
I am standing here in Kousba.
On this narrow, sloped street,
on this October day, I, who don't exist
without this narrow, sloped street,
have become, have sought to become,
this road, this nearby wall, this very sky.
In the presence of such other,
my heart can't find its pulse.
I'm hovering right now above the street.
I'm standing right now on the street.
I'm one of the stones of the street.

The Last Azars in Kousba

My father's village wears me like a brooch,
memento of sons and daughters
lost, stored in the back of a drawer.
The old country. No one says that now.
But this is it, and my aunt in her always black
and I, standing here, are the last,
twin to a single rush of blood
about to set sail for a new world,
the last to stop on this verandah
and scan tiers of olive groves pruned
by a thousand hands.

America is a place of firsts,
an hourglass never turned back.
Countries have emptied themselves
into its dream, and my aunt and I,
we're the last two grains.

Saint George Necklace

First day back in Lebanon,
and it's gone, like a boy soldier

sick for sight of the farm.
Years, it lay kinked in a junk box, old purse.

Rummaging for something,
I'd run smack into its conjuring—

my grandfather's leather valise, his rosary,
the scent of cedar trees, but just.

Alone in that Hamra hotel,

I upend bags, jab pockets,
shake out my fickle satchel's guts, hoping

its stitches will yield
to slip loose the hidden gold.

My Father's Sister

I saw he was given back to me
in her face come down from the mountain.
       My eyes were hers.
Her eyebrows, my youngest sister's,
and then—in her hands that were my father's,
warm and firm of touch, I lost track of home.

       What happened was
              a stitch ripped out clean through.

And once again those dreams, the old house—
we're waiting, my mother and I, for the sound of his car,
and he's so much later than he's ever been.

The House in Kousba

Before I was born I lived in my father's house,
empty now. The veranda swing rusts for love,

unhitches its anyhow limbs. Fruit trees wander.
I've lost his ten-year old self, though I wait

for a boyish lilt or slip of arm.
Surely there's DNA, stuff of eyes and lungs,

grubbed in corners and cracks, the living-remains
scraped up to cut a key to this place, enough

to encode me or embrace me home.
But the house can't recall my name.

The knock of my footstep in the doorway
drums frail air.

Recognizing the Olive

Olive Pickers, those from the Khoura are called.
Cousins gave me oil wrung from trees they own
in a Chivas Regal urn. In my flat, the changeling
jug rendered unction and salvation. Everywhere
I walked were dwarf, gnarled trees jeweled
with dusky fruit. One day, I asked what they were.

Traveling Alone Again

That game we play with kids,
someone disappears
behind a cloth or book,
the dearth of a face so quick,
like waking as usual,
walking, hearing, or seeing as usual
and gone.
                    More than two-bit musing
on matter and nothingness, survival or not,
we, when the face we must have spills
beyond our boundary,

we disappear too,
and the I that remains is the stranger who
can't recall how to feed herself.

Chicago Love Song

(After Badr Shakir al-Sayyab)

If I'd written *Your eyes are two palm groves*
      at the hour of dawn,
the palms would be rooted in my bones.
Wide, feathered leaves would whisper
in the blood, and the greening of the light
of the grove, where once I might have wandered
in the early air of a sleepless Phoenician night,
 would sheen behind my lids.

Are you Lebanese or American?
      I've been asked.
I was born in Chicago, and this is what I know:
That without you I'm a platform of the El
wind-iced at 3:00 a.m.
That together we're a convertible ride
along Lake Shore Drive in June.
That your eyes at dawn, Habibi,
are the bronze Art Institute Lions, both of them.

Expat Story

Loose, wind-borne pages will often land here,
something about the crux of the shore—

lonely men, love's refugees,
American ex-hippies, Indonesian maids,

the Norwegians who stayed despite bombings,
the Afrikaner who told me

It's easy living in Lebanon, because she has a stove.
Will they turn out to be the heroes of their lives?

Each day they plot new twists to unravel every night.
Open the books—another broken heart, another

near escape, and now look, the sun's rising,
just in time. This being both in and out of the body,

subject and object, belonging and not, this way
no one grabs your sleeve, pins you in place.

It's a good fiction, a French novelist tells me,
that travels well.

At Immigration

Pink plastic sandals, little Indonesian maid,
who're these people who've turned you to stone?
I wish I could help, but I can't.

Who has your passport, where's your sad
mother who's sent you so far from home?
Pink plastic sandals, little Indonesian maid,

you're invisible in a language you can't recreate,
iced by the chill of this bureaucrat's throne.
I wish I could help, but I can't

since I too here am pleading my case
through Lebanese cousins trained to cajole.
Pink plastic sandals, little Indonesian maid,

I see you've no friends to aid
you, none to tend bruises, your dead-eyed cold.
I'd like to help you, but I can't.

Others in poems and prayers may complain
they'd fight against slavery this bold,
but pink plastic sandals, little Indonesian maid,
I wish I could help you. I can't.

Ahmed and Me

Ça va? I think I hear a grinning Ahmed ask,
as he drives me from the airport in Beirut.

I've been away. London for a while.

Très bien et vous? I reply, expecting his
"Pas trop mal" tossed out

lifeline-like back to me.
This artless French is all we've had.

What signifies can be a trill of wings,
a crinkled eye, when treasure is sense.

We're dolphins fond of our trainers,
aliens frantically transmitting clicks.

But Ahmed turns blankly away.

My mind rewinds his words: *Ça va?*—how does it go?
and suddenly I hear, it's *Sauvage*.

Ahmed's dream of a swinging West. *Oui, sauvage,*
I say at last, though it's a lie and the moment gone.

Fear, When He's At Home

—Going to the iftar?
—No way, she laughed. *They bomb those places.*

I came into the kitchen and coughed,
six sparrows scrammed from the feeder outside.

Fate miscued day-in day-out tames fear,
something anyhow waiting at the door.

There's this woman with six lumps, innocent all
but the last.

Each year for six years, the shaking phone
leapt from her hand,

each time she flew
less and less far off, until

even the nurse's voice, blank
as the eye of a shark, seemed right.

Oh that, she breathed in and came back,
as she must, to peck at her clutch of seeds.

They say it's the hungriest bird
first to return to the perch,

she who might certainly, one dull day,
find she's the tabbycat's lunch.

Beloved

Hala, first day of class,
told me she wore the hijab by choice,
counted men as friends—

her husband didn't mind. Both of us
had brown hair and eyes, the same
number fingers and toes, the same

bit of goods between our legs.
Like me, she ached at the grace of Sethe's spill
into sin when she slit

her baby's throat, startled
by the face of innocent guilt.
Hala showed me Tripoli, its souks and cafes.

Once, over tea, she reached out
to clasp my hand. Of 9/11 she said,
Surely you know it was Jews.

Eid al-Fatir

Last night of Ramadan and Tripoli's ablaze
like a Times Square Christmas Eve.

Where is the child offered to me
at the iftar for the poor,

the wavy-haired lamb, little dove?
She asks you to take her,

Sadika translates for me,
the mother clutching, pushing out

the girl whose life will be
sacrifice, sacrifice, sacrifice

if I don't.
I want to take her like nothing else,

untie her baby hands from the prickle tree,
crown ribbons upon her head.

I would nestle her beside my infant niece
asleep, born into sin,

dreamful in her cradle of silver and down.

Make-Up Lessons

(University of Balamand, Lebanon)

At the blackboard, I'm rumpled and dun.
To inspire beauty and truth, I ask my students,

must art be beautiful and true?
In the first row, all term, Raja's tried to teach me

the art of maquillage. She's kind and concerned
and after class, suggests a special facial cream,

how to rim my eyes with kohl.
I'm the shabby American, who is also Lebanese,

a woman of the tribe. It's what she'd counsel
a favored aunt, it's mother-to-daughter advice.

Beauty is intimate, she instructs, and pushes me
to pluck my brows blank and write them in clean,

reality and truth are lovers, not friends.
I'm the rhyme she's trying to revise, doggerel

to designer, since poetry, I've lectured,
can make us finer, more alive.

It's a lesson she seems to get,
in her way, and I'm grateful she sees me

worthy of a luminous cheek. *It's about light*,
I tell my class. It can tart up the plainest poem.

Terrorist, Beirut

Everything turns on blood.
You think it doesn't matter,
bread and tea, laughter—

With friends out late,
a young man turned his face, masked
al-Qaeda style in a checkered keffiyeh

to tease at me—*See, I'm a terrorist,*
and I, in kind, became the World Trade Towers,
Abu Ghraib, the occupation of Iraq.

I was rock music, alcohol, drugs,
the great oppressor, the great Satan,
Israel's puppet, American dog.

Yes, I said, smiling. *We're all terrorists now,*
which made him laugh behind his scarf
where I couldn't see his teeth.

To Come Back, to Recall

First thing—tossed all crockery
stored in boxes shuttered in high,
needs-a-stepstool places,

drawers, their characters formed,
forced to reinvent,
knickknacks orphaned and out

and out those five woolen throws,
my hair and arms flying, and out again
you never-used cookbooks, hoarded

just in case. For months,
I'd leaned into the sea
that leaned into the mountain

that framed my small flat:
its two forks, its four plates.
a St. George icon

bartered from a chalkwhite monastery
whose single courtyard jasmine, lacy and sweet,
has for centuries bloomed.

At Home

All day I check the bird feeder
for what's new. If anywhere, it
can happen there. Then, inevitable,
eye pans wide to the beyond,
the neighbor's yard,
his three trees and a shed.

Mine is no original mind.
Let's not pretend.

This, what the lenses give,
tonics and trims like wine,
a game of dice.
Apparently, it's what I choose,
or what is not unchosen,
three trees, a shed,
a paroxysm of sparrows now and then.

Lebanese-Israeli War

(Summer 2006)

Suppose it's the Old God still happy
to wager with his slick homeboy
our lives. Our job, to be played.
Our job, to believe freedom's a dangling purse,

the bush only burns for us, we
who would kill and die for love.
All for His sexy love.
                    So, o.k., then.
Let's say Israel is indeed the promised.
What's He want in trade? What's the game, the hitch,
the pitch, the con? Eye for an eye,

one crushed child's much like all the rest?
Prophecy, fables say, can be tricky, a riddle,
a joke no one broke in time.

Squinting down at His puny brood,
at Qana and Haifa both, surely He must know
He's gonna lose His shirt.

Pilgrimage

(L. *per ager*, through the fields)

Dreaming, I saw that movement is all,
the ends of my coat anteloping as I walked,
worms underground careening, olive trees a collage,
and me too, my feet unstoppable, churning
like the orbiting earth toward what it perceives
is its center, away from its edge.
All this fuss. All this searching.
The sacred asks us please to pack our bags.
I wake each morning amazed to find myself
still in the same place.

Notes

"Coyotes at Balamand": Many Christian families in the north live in the mountains—thus the reference to bread and wine. Muslim families tend to live in the villages below—thus the iftar. An *iftar* is the meal served after sunset all during Ramadan. To feed someone iftar is thought to be a charitable act.

"Chicago Love Song": The word *habibi* is an endearment that comes from the word *habib*, which means beloved.

About the Author

Susan Azar Porterfield was born in Chicago to a southern-belle mother and a Lebanese father. She is the author of two previous books of poetry, including *In the Garden of Our Spines* (Mayapple Press) and *Beirut Redux* (Finishing Line Press). She is also the editor of *Zen, Poetry, the Art of Lucien Stryk* (Ohio UP). She is the recipient of an Illinois Arts Council award for poetry and is currently a Professor of English at Rockford College.

Other Recent Titles from Mayapple Press:

Susan Kolodny, *After the Firestorm,* 2011
        Paper, 62pp, $14.95 plus s&h
        ISBN 978-1-936419-07-4
Eleanor Lerman, *Janet Planet,* 2011
        Paper, 210pp, $16.95 plus s&h
        ISBN 978-1-936419-06-7
George Dila, *Nothing More to Tell,* 2011
        Paper, 100pp, $15.95 plus s&h
        ISBN 978-1-936419-05-0
Sophia Rivkin, *Naked Woman Listening at the Keyhole,* 2011
        Paper, 44pp, $13.95 plus s&h
        ISBN 978-1-936419-04-3
Stacie Leatherman, *Stranger Air,* 2011
        Paper, 80pp, $14.95 plus s&h
        ISBN 978-1-936419-03-6
Mary Winegarden, *The Translator's Sister,* 2011
        Paper, 86pp, $14.95 plus s&h
        ISBN 978-1-936419-02-9
Howard Schwartz, *Breathing in the Dark,* 2011
        Paper, 96pp, $15.95 (hardcover $24.95) plus s&h
        ISBN 978-1-936419-00-5 (hc 978-1-936419-01-2)
Paul Dickey, *They Say This Is How Death Came into the World,* 2011
        Paper, 78 pp, $14.95 plus s&h
        ISBN 978-0932412-997
Sally Rosen Kindred, *No Eden,* 2011
        Paper, 70 pp, $14.95 plus s&h
        ISBN 978-0932412-980
Jane O. Wayne, *The Other Place You Live,* 2010
        Paper, 80 pp, $14.95 plus s&h
        ISBN 978-0932412-973
Andrei Guruianu, *Metal and Plum: A Memoir,* 2010
        Paper, 124 pp, $16.95 plus s&h
        ISBN 978-0932412-966
Jeanne Larsen, *Why We Make Gardens (& Other Poems),* 2010
        Paper, 74 pp, $14.95 plus s&h
        ISBN 978-0932412-959

For a complete catalog of Mayapple Press publications, please visit our website at *www.mayapplepress.com.* Books can be ordered direct from our website with secure on-line payment using PayPal, or by mail (check or money order). Or order through your local bookseller.